Pieces

Kathy Cable Smaltz

PJPF Press

www.piedmontjpf.com

These poems are works of creativity. Names, characters, businesses, places, events and incidents are either the products of the author's imagination or used in a fictitious manner. Any resemblance to actual persons, living or dead, or actual events is coincidental.

ISBN - 13: 978-0-578-22533-3

For my husband and children ... I dreamed of and chose you.
Love is hard work, but oh, those beautiful, precious moments.

"And is it over now, do you know how pick up the pieces and go home?"

-Gold Dust Woman, Stevie Nicks

Part I

The Mississippi
July 2007

We crossed the Mississippi, went West to its muddy waters,
but because we couldn't agree, we turned back East again,
all in one afternoon.

The man who took our family picture didn't know the miles between us.
You, me, and the kids all smiles.
Sometimes I'm fooled too.

Thing is, I'd waited my whole life to see that river.
I wanted to point to it, exclaim, "See? There it is!"
But it looked like any other we'd crossed.

Then I saw the island:
maybe the same one Twain steered the riverboat around,
or where Huck hid when he faked his death.

I can see them:
Huck and Jim, floating, trailing their fingers in the cold water,
hot breeze against their faces, together and alone,
knowing they would pay for their hours of freedom,
that one day the raft would be gone and the ruse over.
But still they did it, and for a minute I felt it too …

If I could just swim to the surface one time,
breathe in the air made for me,
reach out my hand to the endless sky,

my lungs would stop bursting, and
it would be enough to coax me the rest of the way.

Through the Window
(On Observing Room in New York, 1932 by Edward Hopper)

It is one of my favorite paintings, really,
her slumped shoulders and tapping finger.
He reads the paper, leans into its pages and not her arms.

No drinks on the table, nor is her face turned toward him,
rather it's dipped downward into the crook of her own neck,
he is not reading to her, nor is he listening to the stray tap of keys.

Alone in their togetherness.

What You Have to Give

You hate the silver maple that rains helicopters in the spring,
bearing infant trees with tricky roots,
our constant battle between forest and meadow.

It is not my favorite tree for looking, nor any good to climb,
but I love that it's so stubborn and profligate.

I heard once that when a fire burns, it clears the land,
and sometimes what grows back is native to a drier climate:
gone are the maples, replaced by junipers.

Here is Darwin's evolution,
taking root in whatever Earth offers.

As for you and me, I too know how to survive.

When I grow back, it is with fewer needs so
my roots don't search, endlessly,
for water you don't have to give.

Marriage

The litmus test was the clothes hamper.
Those months I slept beside you
but not with you
I started my own pile of dirty laundry
in the back of the closet behind black boots.

It took effort to keep separate,
our summer clothes, but I wanted
no tangled sleeves, trespassing underwear,
no stray sock leading on a pant leg.

When the clothes were clean,
I stuffed some in a suitcase from the attic.
Practical pants, billowing blouses,
folded like tiny parachutes that
could break my fall.

Later, our laundry joined again,
I found the suitcase full of sleeveless silks
and shivered at their lightness.

Part II

Sylvia, Oh Sylvia

First published in *The Piedmont Journal of Poetry & Fiction*

Why were you baking cakes while Ted combed the beach?
Your empty desk with its watery view: endless waves just out of reach.

In the kitchen coated in flour, smelling of vanilla bean,
You greeted Ted with confection, instead of poems, tight and lean.

Like puddles of water trapped in sand after high tide, the madness:
Postpartum. Insomnia. Depression. Diseases of the mind, not mere sadness.

Years later, reading your words, I wish I could save you as you've saved me:
Bound up the stairs, bend over you, blow words into your breathless body.

I want to shake your shoulders, say, "Sylvia! You don't need Ted or any man.
Pick up your pen, push out more poems instead of babies who need prams.

Love what you have, go back to the door, and peel off that silly tape.
Caress your children's cheeks, climb into bed with them. Get. Some. Sleep."

Then – that morning, instead of finding you lifeless, dead,
I would have squeezed you fresh orange juice, made toast, and said:

"These black marauders come and go.
They're matchstick men, not the real foe."

Love and Loathing in the D.M.V. Office
First published in *The Piedmont Journal of Poetry & Fiction*

I am in love with this D.M.V.,
with its beige tile squares and
matching walls with the reassuring
female computer voice who calls
out letter and number combinations,
each random utterance a flutter
in my heart that my turn has come.

I am in love with the black woman
who wears gold hoops and has orange
hair, whose line you stand in to get
your number for the real line so that
when you sit down, you're grateful.

I am in love with the crew cut man
who wears his sunglasses, not on his
head as others do, but above his eyebrows,
whose Nirvana's muscle shirt
takes me back to Kurt Cobain's terrible
pain and the way he sounded live 'cause I
heard him in concert right before he killed himself.

And now I am deeply in love with this mother
to my left who had the nutty notion to bring
all four of her children to this place
presumably because she's got pressing business
and no one else to leave them with.

I am in love with her parenting flaws, the way
she hasn't stopped fussing at them since we all
arrived. "Stop," and "No!" formed on her full
pink lips, blonde hair swept up in a ponytail
like I wear mine most summer days.

I am in love with the way she stands
at the counter now, in her tight denim crop
pants, baby on her hip, his left fist balled into
his mouth, and I am in love with the way they
expected something wonderful to happen
once they got called up, but how so far, nothing has.

I am in love with these numbered
windows and with my turning 40
which is why I'm here, and with
the fact that nothing's changed since
last time I visited the D.M.V. – that in
the midst of war, recession, and Wifi,
we can still count on the sameness of
bureaucracy, a slow room crowded with
so many hapless people, and these hard
plastic chairs whose backs give just a little
bit when you push, stretch, and sigh,
settling in to wait for your number to
be called, while outside these walls, the world
is happy to go on without you.

At Night the Killer in Darkness

(Auvillar, France, 2012)
First published in *The Piedmont Journal of Poetry & Fiction*

Who found the knives
I placed in the French crock last night?
A subtle gesture, each blade brought
down off the magnetic board in darkness
a bit like tucking them in, so I, who am alone
do not wake in fear of being cut.

In America, intruders cut
the phone and electric lines and knife
people in their sleep, those alone
are most vulnerable at night,
where sociopaths love the darkness,
the intimate thrill it brings.

Those Florida college girls even brought
their boyfriends in, years ago, but the killer cut
all of them in the darkness
in a ground floor apartment in Gainesville, a knife
the weapon du jour and night
the perfect cloak for a killer acting alone.

I am afraid of sleeping alone,
and the airlines said no mace, so I bring
myself into the kitchen at night,
where the weak overhead bulb cuts
through black, and there – the knife.
Days ago, across the Atlantic's waves, grey and dark
I sat in my window seat, flew alone,
ate my sesame chicken with my plastic knife.
I didn't know I'd brought
along this killer like carry-on luggage, the predator cut
out from headlines, strongest at night.
I sleep better now at night
knowing that in the darkness
if I'm attacked, I too can cut:
eye, gut, heart of a killer, alone.
He won't be the only one who brought
with him the gleaming blade of a knife.

Once home again, on the news, killers will knife through the darkness
on my flat screen at night, but then I will not be alone
as the glare of our TV is brought into focus, then cut.

On the Banks of the Garonne
(Auvillar, France, August 2012)

This river's thick algae, slows its
surface, makes its current,
near the bank, flat, still. But under-
neath, bubbles pop as oxygen
breathes through the water warm
from summer's heat. Had Nana

painted this, she'd use oil as with
her mill, forest, creek, and waterfall.
I think she'd like I'm here in France,
and I wish she'd done something

like this for herself, but instead she
raised me, and surrendered her
studio to my uncle, when he smashed
his car into a tree, drunk off beer and

vodka. It's hard to speak of this,
for when she died, drowning in her
fluid filled lungs, ten years had passed
since we'd talked. She did her best,

but let me be plain: she wanted to
control us, her love channeled off
for those who complied. When Papa
was dying, she wanted him to last

longer to collect his benefits,
watched him waste away without
a tear. And at his burial she said,

"Good, he's on a hill. He'll be
washed away, worms and all."

I wonder, now, if she might have
been less bitter had she gone to France
like I have, and had a big white
room to call her own. I imagine her now:

painting in oil on rolled out canvases
to capture scenes like this one, where
water bubbles up like a kind of forgiveness flowing between the living and the dead.

Nana

She sold encyclopedias –
had a black leather bag
for the promos – sleek posters,
supplements, special editions,
a swatch of leather bindings.

I remember the clear plastic pages
that fell neatly over the human body
giving it an endocrine system,
adrenal glands, lymph nodes,
nerves, muscles – all the organs
we cannot live without.

She drove every road of each
neighborhood in Allendale,
Mahwah, Ramsey, walked up
flagstone paths, slate sidewalks.
Carried her heavy bag of books
on a permanently stooped shoulder,
The scoliosis in her back
worsening like her mother's.

She must've been good at selling
since she won a trip to Spain.
Her smile wide in those photos,
the colorful, floral print dress
that flounced around her legs.

She was 53 when I was born,
almost my age now.
No wonder she thought she could do it –
I still have young children.

But it ended badly for her.
I wish I could convince her at 50
not to raise the baby, to instead live
out her dreams of retirement.

Rather than a second go at carpools,
Halloween costumes, and clarinet lessons,
she should've squeezed more

pastel tubes onto pallets, painted
more mountains.

I'm seeing now you can't
put life off without a price,
and hers was too high:
giving up art and a quiet house,
sinking social security and
pension into braces.

She did this for me, I guess.

But she was also cruel
like it was something she'd studied
in one of those encyclopedias
that lined our shelf.

How to clip a girl's wings
so she won't fly away.

Daffodils

Now that you're dead,
you speak to me through
your paintings –

the watercolor bird clinging to
a clementine,
its white eye accusing;

a still life I remember
hanging on our wall
at home – the goblet's

shading makes it look
as though it is cut
from onyx or jade

a contrast to the
porcelain pitcher,
a sliced cantaloupe,

half on plate,
half on table
next to a lemon.

In the third painting,
the quiet of winter is all I hear:
silence punctuated by
the groaning of tree limbs
weighted down with snow,

like the last time I saw you:
my goodbye forever
your dismissal of me
a half-turned body.

No one had ever left you before I
drove away that day, resolute, freed,
but still bound by our unforgiving.

Like your canvases,
these poems I write all
different lyrics to

the same melody, as if
each iteration
of my girlhood self

has to rise up: as if
I were the one buried, not you.

Let us forgive with this last:
four daffodils on
straight, green stems
reaching strong, high,
petals bright with sun.

Part III

A Good Memory of Mom

I was five when
my mom and I first
circled that pond
where ducks glided
across the smooth
surface, and we fed them
bread ends and crusts
from the bag.

In stories, swans
were more beautiful,
but in life, ducks' feathers
glistened on the ground,
and I -- too young to know
she wouldn't always
be with me, still stuffed
my pockets full.

Pieta

Yes, I was folded up into him
like my arms and his legs
made one person and this,
after we'd just met on a PATH bus,

pulling out of Port Authority headed
to Passaic, and yes, we were only 16
and in my cousin's backyard on her
patio furniture with its floral patterns
swirling fuzzily because we were drunk
on adrenaline and teenage lust.

Yes, I was too boy-crazy and maybe
French kissing was a lot like intercourse,
like Nana told me, the boy's tongue
searching out my pink mouth, precursor
to his penis seeking out the pink of my vagina,
lips parting, but I had never done more than kiss
and be kissed, grope and be groped, still innocent
to the internal bruising of true penetration.

But also, this trip to Manhattan was made
to bring me closer to God – to the chapels
of St. Patrick's, where I kneeled in front of
marble saints, untainted, and asked forgiveness
anyway, to bring me closer to the truth –
to the Barbizon Modeling School
where at 16, my mother walked in straight lines
imagining books stacked on her head,
her hair as straight as her back,
this mother I knew only as an addict, a patient,
an object of pity.

Meanwhile, back at the cathedral –
Mary, true mother, cradled her grown son, Jesus –
when his body was taken down from the cross,
and all I wanted was to climb up the steps,
lie down in her arms, and be held like Him,
but that would be embarrassing,
really, and illegal –
security called, I escorted out, ashamed.

Better to climb into the lap
of this boy who called to me,
whose smiling eyes said,
in the reflection of bus windows,
come, be the object of my compassion.

Feeling Better

So I go out on the porch
for a smoke, but I don't smoke
so instead I sit
next to this man who does.

He doesn't know this, but
I spent my girlhood on another front porch
inhaling second-hand smoke
at the right side of my mother.

She liked Marlboro Lites, gold foil
cellophane, not cardboard;
I liked pulling the red plastic thread
at the top that pulled the pack open.

Hours passed on that porch while
she exhaled a bitter perfume
and I shared news of school,
crushes on boys, how I did on
my math quiz.

Tonight, this man's so young,
just beginning. He confesses
he has no plan, just ideas
and visions of life in Jacksonville.

I confess I'm 44 and was too
responsible at his age so I don't
recommend it. I am ancient
in his eyes, as I'd have been to my
30 year old self.

Mom was 30 when we sat on the porch
and she asked if I wanted a cigarette.
Shocked, I said, "No!"
"Good girl," she said and lit hers up,
the glowing end of it red with life.

Maybe it was the quiet way this man
asked if anyone wanted to join him
for a cigarette on the porch that made me say sure.

He said he liked hammocks –
not to sleep in, but just to relax and think,
and it made me think of all the hammocks
I've longed to lie down in.
(How hard can it be to find two suitable trees?)

He said he's between things
and that maybe it's finally time
to settle down, maybe he wants
to choose, fall in love, commit.

At his age, I'd been married and teaching
seven years, gone back to grad school,
read War and Peace, and had a
miscarriage. In that order.

I remember that palpable feeling
of time in my hands. And the clear
outlines of dreams still within easy reach.
And now I wonder if my mom felt the same way.

Would tomorrow be the day
they'd make a magic med for her manic
depression – one that didn't pickle her liver,
or make her eyes glaze over
and her body bloat?

Would she be free one day of her own
bag of tricks – beer, whiskey, nicotine?
When the money ran out, instead of
quitting, she bought her own white filter
paper and rolled her own cigarettes,
her index fingers and thumbs turning brown.

And here's something I've never said before:
she wanted to try e-cigs, Vapes, but she didn't
have the cash, I said I'd look into it, but I didn't,
and she died two years later to the day.

It was smoking, in the end, she wouldn't give up.
Not booze, not drugs, not men. Cigarettes.
As she struggled to breathe, her fingers fumbled
for the cellophane pack in her purse,

a purse that's now stuffed in the back of my
clothes closet, not because – peeling pleather and
lint filled lining – it's worth keeping, but because
it was hers, the last thing she touched, they say,
before she died.

So when I go out on the porch
for a smoke, and I don't smoke,
I almost enjoy inhaling that
bitter perfume. I do.

Gypsy Woman

She was a sort-of gypsy, my mom,
wore broom skirts and bangles
on her wrists, waist-length hair
splayed out as she spun.

With her, I learned to sing
into one end of a jump rope,
Stevie Nicks' throaty voice
a melodic undercurrent.

There were other nights though,
when she'd go out to dance, pause
for a drink, wipe one palm, face down
on the smooth polish of the bar.

On those nights, I sang by myself,
played her *Rumors* album, the one
with pony-tailed Mick reaching out
to hold Stevie's hand, both of them
young and beautiful.

She wanders the universe now,
knows more than she did before.

I see her riding the tail of a comet,
young and beautiful again
her skirt billowing, her bracelets
bangling, her hair splayed out behind her,
singing with me again, somehow,
for all the times I sang alone.

Earl Cleans House

I imagine the bright flames
moving in syncopated rhythm
lilting left, then right
like the full skirts of flamenco
dancers. Also, the fire must
have leapt up, impossible
to contain once it took hold,
a green garden hose
hanging limply over Earl's hand,
his thumb poised, ready to make
the water jet, if flames threatened
the shingled roof.

He burned the flea-infested
furniture: the grey couch where
three generations of our women
sat together for a photo one
Sunday after church.
I can see the upholstery
melt away like peeling back
the layers and the synthetic
guts of the couch snorted
like cocaine, chemicals a catalyst
for more frenzied flames burning blue.

The couch was cheap, after all,
but what of the oak Missionary
rocker, its wide armrests worn
smooth these past 100 years?
To survive the flu pandemic and
two world wars just to be burned by
Earl, whose thumb is still ready to propel
water as if one paltry stream could
combat 20 years of neglect.

Maybe I'm coming at this all wrong.

Maybe the burning was more like a
sacrifice, the front yard's crab grass
scorched in an uneven circle, the altar.
Maybe instead of being a squatter

with no rights to our land, Earl is
more of a prophet, God's messenger,
and this bonfire - burnt offerings of
my family's furniture - cleanses us all,
the weak stream of water now aimed
at the fire's feet – a baptism.

Maybe this is what we ourselves ought
to have done: gathered what we thought
was sacred, lit a match, and watched it burn,
our belongings like apocrypha, symbols of
our own broken bodies laid out to rest,
rolling into the crematory, skin melting,
peeling back the layers, the smell of
burning hair contained in the furnace,
our heavy bones burned down,
at last, to dust.

If

You're twelve
and your mother
gets driven away
at 5AM in winter darkness
three hours before the first
bell rings at your school,
you don't tell your
homeroom teacher why
you are tired, that your
Mom had a breakdown.

Later, when you're told she'll
be gone for a month, maybe two,
you are angry, because
she was taking you
shopping for a dress
that afternoon, one to
wear at the Seventh
Grade Spring Fling
and now your father
will have to instead.
Not only is he color
blind, he doesn't even
know you wear a bra.

In her absence, the gifts arrive
on the altar of your dresser
like burnt offerings.

Ceramic bowl, good
place for earrings,
painted horse, knick knack on
your shelf: as therapy,
Mom takes Arts and Crafts
like it's camp, sends trinkets
home with your father
who visits on Saturdays.
You tell him you want
to go too, you insist,
so he takes you.

The elevator goes high,
your stomach goes low,
padded walls, blue cushion foam,
doors ping, you step out,
meet beige walls ... sedative one;
then the orderly walks her
to the lounge where you sit
on the edge of a frayed couch,
you see right away
she's on a high
dose of lithium ... sedative two.

This is, in fact, not your mother
at all, this woman whose glass eyes
don't blink, whose smile is vacant,
she even walked into the room all wrong,
glided like a holograph, or a
flat paper doll moved by the hand
of a child.

You wish you could
give her a Marlboro, Gold filter,
or shove her straight
in the chest and yell,
"Wake up! Where are you?"

Your father is sorry he said yes,
you could come.
For it's scary to have a crazy mother
who yells into winter darkness,
and throws table knives into the snow,
who sees what's not there,

but it's far worse for her
to see you, who are there,
but not see you, not at all.

Part IV

Jersey Rain

For me, the Jersey rain is Newark:
potholed pavement on Raymond Street at 1:00AM,
closed ramps, detours, Jersey rain on my windshield,
the wipers squeak, darkness blacker yet off 15E,
abrupt release from airport lights, wrong turn
I knew was wrong but at least was certain:
Newark's Municipal Waste Plant,
trucks passing us by, taking the city's trash
to towering incinerators or a
vast dumping ground too distant to see,
but like the one at home.

Speaking of home, Jersey rain is home too –
not here in Newark, not now, but before I was born,
my heart beat in Jersey rhythms, an hour away.
I keep coming back as if I were the
droplets of rain themselves, pooling in puddles,
soaking in – slowly into the dirt beneath,
disappearing into the Jersey air
forming into clouds, sometimes angry and dark,
sometimes light and thinly stretched, but always
returning as Jersey rain.

For me, Jersey rain is childhood summers,
cotton candy sweetness in carnival air,
ferris wheel lights, circling through hot, black night,
listening to Thriller, teaching younger cousins
to mimic Michael's moves, making divets
in my aunt's front lawn with our moonwalk feet.

Jersey rain the Ramapos too, the diamond clad
copperheads crawling out from rock crevices,
forbidden from crossing the street to Russell's house
where his yard backed up to the rock face.

Jersey rain falls on this Virginia girl, never
native to the South, more like one of those
exotic pets people buy for novelty, then flush
down toilets or push out of moving cars into
weedy ditches. Never native there walking

in tobacco fields where canopy leaves
went to seed, hitchhikers stuck onto hems.

Virginia rain unlike Jersey rain,
fell at a slant driven by wind into the
screens of our house where we were planted without
roots, like taking a non-native plant
hoping it will not just grow but flourish,
finding it doesn't, all wrong for the red clay.

For me, Jersey rain is a kind of fear tipped
over from my heart's bucket, suspended in
the sky with the light dark clouds, cousins of who I
could have been, once was, want to be, and find
to my surprise, I am.

Part to Whole
First published in *The Piedmont Journal of Poetry & Fiction*

Each year I find more of myself
up and down the banks of this river.

Ashamed of who I was back then,
I filleted myself like a fish, cut
through the flapping tail while
bulging eye stared, blade sliced
through spine and scales
then guts spilled out, heart
beating, bleeding, offering up
only the parts men told me they'd eat.

Over here behind the boat,
given up for you,
two bared breasts, no big deal
just teenage A cups with tender pink tips,
but they were mine and I peeled
them off, replaced with silicon
so someone would say he remembered me.

I once watched a friend fillet
fish on his dock, the S shaped motion of the
knife, accusing eye watching,
I asked him why he let them
suffer like that
why he didn't behead them
first but he said fish don't suffer because
they don't know, and no one cuts the head
off if he knows what he's doing it's bloody
and wasteful, only done in cinema, better
the head and tail go down together
without their body into the chum bucket
or back into the river.

If you crouch on your hands and knees
under that cleaning table, you'll find my heart,
with all of its severed valves, just where I hid it
hoping, one day, to return for my broken treasure.

I no longer remember why these
faceless men mattered more to me
than I mattered to me
except my sense of self so shrunken from shame
I couldn't name, or know its source.
I miss that girl sometimes, the one
whose individual body parts, so lovely,
formed a whole so guileless to everyone
but her. She lives inside this older version
of me, inside my beating heart, my fingers, my
breasts, my stretch marked stomach,
my shoulders, my cheeks, my open eyes,
my one true body.

Spring

I.
On this cold March morning
a blackbird's beak digs into
wet dirt, yesterday's snow
melted into mud
makes the worms an easy meal.
Not as many people are writing
nature poems these days, the poet
says after intriguing me with what
her heart knows of the moon,
so I write of the bird in my backyard
that digs in front of our
children's old swingset,
that mausoleum of memories
standing derelict except for
the red Tonka Lego truck on top,
sentinel of their lost world of play.

My youngest son went out briefly –
to sled down the steep hill
behind the church, and I pressed
my footprints down into its fine white field
heel to toe, that crunching sound
only made in packing snow.

If my grandchildren ever ask me
what sounds I loved most in my youth,
I will tell them this
one was my favorite, for it spoke of beginnings.

II.
On patchy yellow forsythia,
red breasted robins dart from
branch to branch, snow below them
cold on their feet.

I try, but fail, for a photo, contrast of
Spring and Winter – one season groaning
into life while the other dies.

It is only when unwelcome Winter
holds onto life, clinging long past
its time, that I mourn how little I gave
myself to her.

III.
We made it through winter
we all say, as though these
dark months didn't shield us
from Spring's desire and
Summer's wanton despair.
We are quick to forget the way winter –
in its chasing us indoors –
offered us quiet reflection,
an excuse to disengage.

IV.
My son started the bottom of
a snowman, but kept on rolling
fifty yards, leaving in his wake
a bright green swath.
Now a haystack of snow stands
testament to our Spring miracle
and I watch it shrink, refreeze each day.

V.
The fake cloth flowers
on my kitchen table
speak of Spring – that
grand masquerade –
and each year that passes,
we, the willing procession,
pretend we do not know,
speak not of our necessary losses.

Dandelions

They stand straight, tall, as if at attention, white
fuzzy helmets on the heads of
spindly soldiers spaced out, rank and file.

No one wants them – they're a weed,
unless perhaps when fringed yellow
manes, but never when they go to seed, turn white –

Loved then only by children who make wishes and blow
scattering seeds far and wide – too many to uproot
multiplying into platoons, companies, batallions.

But here, now, they look like polished white marble:
headstones in patriotic rows of fallen dead.

Death knells ringing in the wind
and husks waving on tubular stalks
bending closer to us with the breeze, beckoning.

Wildflowers Have Their Own Appeal
First published in *The Fredericksburg Literary and Art Review*

Wildflowers have their own appeal –
Scruffy bunches scattered 'round more civilized tulips, lilies.
Weren't these ruffians once the only kind of flowers?

Messy majesty, tussled tendrils make
Crazy flower crowns.
Wildflowers have their own appeal.

Before the English gardens –
Neat, clipped, tamed rows, alternating plants and space
Weren't these ruffians once they only kind of flowers?

Unruly lovers of the nature that bred them
Seeds strewn about by orgies of wind and pollen
Wildflowers have their own appeal.

Wildflowers appeal to our sense of freedom.
No one asks them, "Who do you think you are?"
Weren't they once the only kind of flowers anyway?

These flowers sometimes mistaken for weeds,
Unworthy bedfellows, primordial persistence through cracks
Wildflowers have their own appeal for once,
They were the only kind of flower.

Mother, Daughter, and Dark Hollow Falls

(Shenandoah National Park, Spring 2018)

I.
Little girl
poised on the rock of
adolescence, a white
ribbon of water cascades
behind her, its centuries
of secrets beat a
smooth path down this
mountain. We all make this
journey. One step closer
to death, two steps closer to life.

II.
While I write
she sketches
what she witnesses
catching on the page with
her pencil light descending
behind the rocks.

III.
Neither of us, though, can
capture the sound of gushing
water, once a burble,
now a steady roar that will
exhaust itself in the Bay
after its own travels.

IV.
The sun sets, leaves us
shivering on these cold stones.
I am halfway through
my life as she begins hers.
We are each a waterfall.

Riptide

Imagine sleeping in your bed
cool blue walls morph in darkness
waves crash down upon your head
undertow hobbles, no longer harmless.

Cool blue walls morphed in darkness
rip current pulls, shore ever distant
undertow hobbles, no longer harmless
pointless kicks, tired limbs, hoarse yells.

Rip current pulls, shore ever distant
eyes open without sight
pointless kicks, tired limbs, hoarse yells
muscle memory lends death more might.

Eyes open without sight
body flips, cartwheels, flails
muscle memory lends death more might
if instead you could remember not to fight,

Body flips, cartwheels, flails
underwater screams swallow sea
if instead you could remember not to fight
piercing pain where breath should be.

Underwater screams swallow sea
waves crash down upon your head –
piercing pain where breath should be,
imagine sleeping, then you're dead.

Part V

Hercules, a Hero for all Time, Takes Hippolyte's Belt

Hera whispered madness into Hercules' ear,
so he murdered his wife and children.
Who is to blame for this chaos and slaughter?

When I was in high school I translated
the Twelve Great Labors from Latin into English,
Hera whispering madness into Hercules' ear.

Never did I question the slaying of Hippolyte
or the stealing of her belt, didn't identify with the Amazons.
Who is to blame for the chaos and slaughter?

I never admired the women warriors for slicing
off their right breasts so they could better throw a spear.
Hera whispered madness into the Amazons' ears,

telling them to fight for their queen before she was carried
off, so they advanced on Hercules and his men.
Who is to blame for this chaos and slaughter?

When Hercules killed Hippolyte, where was her father, Ares
who had given her the belt in the first place?
Hera whispered madness into Hercules' ear, but
was there another to blame for this chaos and slaughter?

Single Bed

I sleep in the narrow bed alone.
I've shed several skins so I
can fit in here neatly:
Good wife, co-dependent, victim.

Little girls sleep in singles,
and now that I'm finally grown,
it's strange to be back in
a bed that disallows stretching out, owning it.

Last night, my left arm pinwheeled –
struck the wall where the bed rests.
Every time I shifted to fit, the metal
frame squeaked.

I made more noise, alone, in this single,
sleeping, than he and I did in our
marital bed these past months.

There's something I like about the single:
it says, I am one person. I know what I'm about.

Sleeping alone in a queen
can be lonely, especially if
someone else used to shift
his weight on the other side.

But in a single, I can be myself.
I'm not waiting for a man to arrive
like a damsel
in a romance novel.

I am my own hero:
I rescue myself.

Turtle's Shell

I want to be a turtle –
house on my back at all times,
long neck protruding out,
testing the air for security,

taking cover from the things
life lobs at me –
a little slow maybe, less mobile
than my non-terrapin friends

but with the hard shell a woman
needs sometimes to protect
an otherwise vulnerable underbelly.

Sometimes a turtle's shell isn't
enough to protect it though – last night
on my evening walk, I saw a
shattered shell, beautifully bashed

by a ton of fast-moving metal,
its pattern like a shaken kaleidoscope
exploded into a thousand shards like
stars scattered across the asphalt sky.

Like most of us, it was blindsided:
sent reeling onto its soft underside,
its body squeezed out of its shell,
made one dimensional, flattened
onto the road so its head was not
distinguishable from its tail,
its tiny claws the only body part
I could rightly tell, aside from

that brilliant shell of bone and keratin,
fused to its body like our own vertebrae,
yellow-orange speckled beauty,
breathtaking even in death.

That shell speaks to me, saying
beauty is passing and truth broken

into pieces even when both look
whole, untouched.

Hate Poem
(after Julie Sheehan)
First published in *The Piedmont Journal of Poetry & Fiction*

I hate you. Truly I do.
Everything about me hates everything about you.
The tapping of my fingers hates you.
That black speck of pepper that gets caught in my teeth hates you.
The cracking of my phalanges hates you.
Each cochlear ring in my inner ear hates the creak the bed makes when you
turn over in your sleep.
Look out! Horn blaring! I hate you!

The chipped nail polish on my pinky toe hates you.
The topaz geometric ring on my left index finger hates you.
The tension in my forehead as I listen to you say you can't understand
psychology, and thus relationships, hates you.
My hair follicles hate you. Also my uterus.

My blue wrist vein as I squeeze this pen tightly to write you out of my system
hates you.

My clipped words in response to your complaints about your AMEX debt:
hate.
My obligatory hello as you follow the kids into the kitchen: hate.
My silence before I go to our bedroom alone: hate.
You know how I peak into a room to see if you're there before I go in? Hate.
The Nutter Butter cookies I bought for you, then forgot about, then gave you
three days ago? Hate.
My turning off the overhead light in the spare room where you now sleep,
replacing it with the dimness of a lamp? Also hate.
Layers of hate, shedding like dead skin.
Hours after our latest fight, the tiny muscle in the bridge of my nose twitches,
the long thick straps of muscle in my abdomen begin to release their
stranglehold of hate,
The hammock of my heart begins to beat a slower rhythm, a funeral dirge to
our once love.
The drum of my left inner ear thuds in time to the pulse of blood sent out by
my aorta, the biological proof of how much I loathe you.

Saturday Afternoon
(Manassas Junction)

I've been leaving a long time now.
These railroad tracks, if you follow them
South six miles, run right past our house
and what is our home but a boilerplate
of my becoming the one that leaves?

Bookcases brimming with titles on how
to love yourself more, novels full of
cheating wives, unseeing husbands,
a café table with two chairs I bought
but you never wanted – always trying
to write the tale of a romantic couple
in love with the same narcisstic vision,
but I became more you than me.

These railroad tracks would carry me
to Richmond, if I let them, where perhaps
I could unspool the thread to trace my
obsession with living alone,
accountable only to myself, lonely,
yes, but also giddy with the freedom
I bought by giving you up, by
boarding the next train out of here.

Today it is quiet – no commuter cars,
fewer travelers use these as through tracks;
the cacophony created by wood thrush
and lark, not the mighty rumble of steel
on steel cobbled together by wooden ties,
not the hiss of brakes and madness of
whistle and horn, just the quiet voices
of families happier than ours walking
over the empty tracks and my sometimes
sadness as it explodes from my heart
asking if self-reliance will heal it
or hurt it more.

Refrigerator

The old one hummed and thrummed
for a dozen years or so before the
day we noticed the lukewarm milk.

My husband, a handyman, checked
its pulse, diagnosed its ailment
and set about fixing it
like he does with most things.

Meanwhile, we'd moved the ham,
four bottles of salad dressing, the
milk --- among other sundries – to
our back up fridge in the mudroom.

He resuscitated that old fridge
breathed life back into its lungs
so we moved everything back
relieved of the new appliance expense.

But within the week, it had
failed again so I started
pricing a new one – stainless steel
instead of white.

A few days before, the men delivered
the new fridge my daughter and I peeled
off the magnetized memories.
Some went back years:
toothless baby, sun bleached toddler curls,
first grade football pose,
the magnets told a story of our journeyed past.

What I wonder now is how hard
should we try to fix
what we've got? It's just the right size,
we're used to it, it's paid for. How many times
should we blow our life-giving air into the
cooling lips, push down on the
chest of a dying thing?

It's easier, I think, to look askance,
go online, and choose a new one,
but if I'd known that the top shelf
was half the size because of the light
and that my butter wouldn't fit
in its allotted space nor my magnets
stick to the steel, I'd have asked to try again –

Just one more time, please
do that thing you did before,
let's hold our breaths, wait, and see.

Flight

I.

I search for houses I can
afford without getting the
divorce. They don't amount to
much these houses, outdated,
small, some in need of major
renovation or a creative vision.

To move on with my life
means terminating the old.

Half our dishes in my rented
townhome, half back at our house
we've reached a stalemate,
separation merely a mirror of
our misguided marriage.

II.

I need movement, any kind an
improvement over this stagnancy.

I am like my childhood self
in a game of summer evening freeze tag,
touched on the shoulder in the
yard's periphery, then forgotten by It in a
scramble to tag more runners,
dutifully standing still,
following the rules of a game
no one else follows and that I
no longer wish to play.

III.

Last week, I dreamed our oldest daughter
fell on a bird pecking seed off the sidewalk.
When I helped her to her feet,
I looked at the ruined bird beneath
whose wings popped off and lay
separately on the cement --

useless but beautiful feathers
no longer fit for flight.

IV.

Somehow, in the wake of our flight,
our marital house is like a museum,
the left behind books in the living room lay
scattered on the coffee table I wanted but was
too bulky to take, the kids' Legos left
right where they'd lived under the beds, now
exposed in fluorescent light. We took what
was easy, what we could carry:
prized pandas, long loved loveys,
the pillows and blankets smelling
of their sweat. What fit into my mini-van,
a friend's short bed truck.
Birds toppling out of a nest
falling fast to concrete, beating wings
just in time to escape impact.

Part VI

Gangrene

At the end, my aunt's foot
grew black with gangrene -- first
the big toe, then the rest, so brittle
I feared they'd break off in the bed
fall off like rotting teeth,
this first death a foretaste of the rest.

I liked to keep her foot covered
with the pilled blanket, hidden
from our children who had seen death
only in its aftermath, not in its coming,
great grandma, made up in her casket, and
the closed coffin of a ten year old classmate,
who'd been killed on his dirt bike.

Gangrene was -- to me -- only a page in our
first aid book junior year of high school --
the result, our teacher said, of a person
suffering so bad a wound
that a tourniquet was needed --
the tourniquet, he said, can save a life
to halt bleeding, but use only if you are
certain because you could cut off
circulation to the limb too long, thereby sacrificing it.

When I was a kid, I played with Barbies
and our dog sometimes chewed off the rubber
foot of a doll I left on the floor.
To see a foot the size of my thumb lying there,
severed from its leg, caused me distress
but now, thirty years later, to see my aunt's foot
decaying .... death starting in the cells
as it always does, but visible,
blackening her skin, wrapping its
fingers around each of her toes,
strangling one after another, then her foot, then
her ankle, creeping death -- a proclamation
that it will take you too, one day, ready or not.

Involuntary Reflexes

My friend is dead.
At the end, we thought
she was thirsty, but we
couldn't give her water since
she could have drowned in
the fluid of her own lungs.

Eight days without food or water,
and her body lay there
in the hospital bed
dressed in the white gown
they give you to die.

Her hair lost its lustre
her skin turned pallid, then ash grey,
sometimes her lips puckered like
she wanted a kiss or to latch
as if -- before crossing over -- she were
regressing to infancy.

Her hand, warm and moist for a few days,
her forehead set in a thinking scowl as if
she were hard at work puzzling out answers.
Her bosom a soft pillow where we
laid our heads whispering our
last words of love.

The dying seldom speak.
After many years of
trying to choose the right words,
suddenly there are none.
The living listen to messages
the almost dead left on their loved ones'
phones days or weeks before
just to hear their voices again.

They tell us they love us, call back soon.

What's good about dying
is the letting go, I think,
'cause I'm not dead yet or dying.

My friend is dead.
At the beginning we thought
surgery could save her,
piece back together torn walls,
but the brain is trickier
than the heart.
The heart lets you repair it
sometimes
but the brain seldom does.

Her brain grew into a maze of
twists and turns, dead ends,
shredded pathways, tangles.
It started with the forgetting.
Grew with the headaches.

At the end, we thought she'd
returned. She brought her hand
up to her cheek, scratched an itch.

The doctor said, "involuntary reflexes."

To watch her lie motionless
for days on end then scratch her cheek
filled us with useless hope.

There is no logic in love.
Just involuntary reflexes.

Italian Bird Song for Jan
(Memorial Day Weekend, 2017)

My friend, more like my mother, flies now like a bird.
In her brain, tangles grew, bound her to land,
when she, who always soared, glided high, now unmoored.

Years before, her son died, and she later heard his voice
in bird-song, cheery melodies, all those days unseen.
My friend, more like my mother, flies now like a bird.

The disease dismantled day by day, her nested memories lay
by weakened walls, without warning, burst forth bleeding.
But now, she, who always soared, glides high again, unmoored.

She was at first my mentor, a wise teacher, who brought me to my first
poetry reading. Do you have wind like that beneath your wings?
My friend, more like my mother, flies now like a bird.

Together we talked, taught, attended plays, readings, the opera.
When she lost her son, we became her family, my kids her grandkids.
Now she, who always soared, glides high again, unmoored.

When birds fly high on mountaintops and wind blows cold and strong,
I see her, feel her, honor her, and so in this her song
my friend, more like my mother, flies now like a bird,
where she, who always soared, glides eternally, unmoored.

Sweater

I'm wearing my aunt's sweater,
one of the dozen she gave me
before she died, knowing she was dying,
one sweater at a time, each month
I'd visit. Take them, she said, and I told
her she'd need them for winter; it was
October in New York, the last of the red
maple leaves blazing from the nursing home
window, her prison of safety and solitude.

She'd made it this far, after all, not dead yet,
but her hallucinations from medication,
growing in length and number, her
medication for the diabetic gangrenous toes,
then foot, then ankle, the black of
deadened flesh, cut off from the blue of
life-giving blood, spreading, spreading,
up her leg.

All I could do was cover her up,
pretend it wasn't so.

The nurses, the doctor, the sisters,
all of them said there's nothing we can do.

Have the pink cashmere sweater, she said,
I don't need it, I told her, but to my protest she said
the sisters would descend on it all when she died,
better take it now, and I couldn't believe nuns
would do that and I didn't want to accept she
was really, finally dying.

And this bequeathing of what had kept her warm,
was her holding my hand,
was her cradling my head in her lap,
the blue of her eyes so like mine,
was her encircling my body with her body,
the age spot on her lip that wouldn't go away,
her knuckles twisted, swollen joints,
her thin wrists and warm smile,
her pink skin so smooth from staying out of the sun

her flat breasts like two wafers at Eucharist,
all these parts of her that she wore in life, like this
sweater that I took from her when she shivered in her bed,
no longer able to get it on or take it off,
all these parts of her like a gift to me that I knew not yet,
pieces of herself given freely, without question to feed me
for all the times in the future when she no longer could.

Again

Again the ocean laps at my feet,
tugging on my toes, pulling me closer.
At this beach, white crests of water
silence the noise of this year's
sacrifice – flat, blue-grey sea
seeming to disappear on the horizon.

It is always like this.

Five pelicans soar, then dip.
What they take and eat,
once living, writhes no more
just like the soft bodies
that once lived in these hard
seashells –
where we find beauty,
death has visited.

Is was always like this.

And so I watch a white sail
as far as my eye can see,
sure that the expansiveness
to which I surrender myself
leads on to another place
I cannot imagine –
shifting sand by the tide the one
thing that, in its changing, stays the same.

Roosevelt Lake

Quiet on the lake
this morning, marshy grasses
thick at its shore where water laps
against the weed choked bank.

Sycamores seek sun at 45 degree
angles, stretch out to the blue-grey
shallows where the wind dances with
the sun's reflection, a mad mirage in scherzo.

A woodcock calls, perched in pine
on alert for fish not far
from the lines where we cast:
our orange bobbers float
while we too watch and wait.

Upstream
August, 2017

Upstream, these are the things I lost:
a pair of navy blue shoes,

the fingernail on my right pinky,
my way.

Here, at the Mississippi Headwaters
rushing currents that wind their
way 1000 miles or more

have to start somewhere --
why not begin as a raindrop
in Lake Itasca?

Looking for something bigger
than myself, I start at the source.

The mighty river Huck rode with Jim --
starts with a lake in Minnesota
not unlike other lakes.

To find myself again,
I paddle, change my pace,
see that the water doesn't

always flow straight, and
sometimes I get stuck on a
sandbar or in an eddy.

90 days later, I find myself
downstream, at the mouth,
in the estuary where
river meets Gulf,

their joint currents moving us all
where they will.

Acknowledgements

First and foremost, I'd like to thank my husband, Mark, who has supported my writing from the early days of attending MFA readings at George Mason University through driving our then young children to Charlottesville on Easter Sunday so we could be together one day out of my 2-week residency at the Virginia Center for the Creative Arts (VCCA), to the more recent handling of playing weekend taxi-cab driver to our now older kids while I slip away to near and far coffeehouses, libraries, lakeshores, mountainsides, and beaches all in the name of writing, revising, editing, and begging the Muses to visit to start the cycle again.

Secondly, thank you to our children who never complain when I tell them not to knock on the door unless it's a real emergency or that I'm dragging them along to another reading. I also want to thank both Mark and the kids for inspiring me... sometimes, they are the subjects or supporting cast in my work since they are the most important people in my life, and I am so blessed to have such a wonderful family.

I'd also like to thank extended family, Aunt Marion, and Jan Suppa-Friedman, Janice Smaltz and Donald Smaltz for being the best in-laws and grandparents ever, Michael Friedman, Jessica and Nick Smaltz and their sons for sharing their lives with us. Thanks also to our "village" of friends and neighbors without whom I could not function quite so highly much less write. Thanks too to my former current and past employers at Prince William County Schools, especially Jack Parker, Robert Scott, and Eric Worcester, for understanding that my life as an artist is integral to my life as a teacher.

Thank you to my two writing groups and countless writer friends with the Northern Virginia Writing Project, without whom I would not have grown as a poet, and to the Project itself who continually renews, inspires, and challenges me. Thanks to aforementioned VCCA for the gift of time, studio space, and a scholarship to write in Auvillar, France and to the Mid-Atlantic Arts Council for the pivotal 2008 grant.

A special thanks to Cathy Hailey who has been there every step of the way, and to Krista Shellenberger - without whom I'd have stalled out and had a lot less fun. To Stacy Shaw for being my friend when I needed one the most and to both her and her husband, Jason, for giving me a chance as a columnist with their online paper, *Bristow Beat*. I can't thank my writer friends - Krista, Robert, Sara, Cindy, Scott, or Milt enough for reading, re-reading, and giving me countless tips on my writing these past 10 years. Thank you to John and Alice for encouraging me to read at Spilled Ink and to shoot for the stars, and thanks to Christine for keeping me sane and making me laugh with two feet on the ground.

Finally, I'd like to thank Piedmont Press and my editor, Sara Brooks, whose intuition and skill were key in the shaping of this collection. I brought her a pile of poems on a rainy night, and thanks to her, themes emerged and patterns took hold. Thanks to all of the poets who've offered support over the years: Sharon Olds, Jennifer Atkinson, Erik Pankey, Ann Shalaski, Sharon Dolan, E. Ethelbert Miller, Carolyn Kreiter-Foronda, Ed Lull, and Bill Glose. I have found the poetry writing community to be full of not only talented artists whose voices inspire me but also generous souls who share their wisdom and joy of life through their words and their friendship. No thanks would be complete without gratitude to Richard Bausch who is a gifted storyteller and professor and to the late Alan Cheuse who held the bar high both in his own writing and in what he expected from his students and whose voice I still hear when I know I need to keep working to get it right.

Kathy Smaltz
Nokesville, Virginia
May, 2019